Matters of the Heart

A One Year Bible Reading Plan & Words To Enrich Journal
Read, Study and Be Inspired

Matters of the Heart

ONE YEAR BIBLE READING PLAN

January

1. Genesis 1-3	Matthew 1
2. Genesis 4-6	Matthew 2
3. Genesis 7-9	Matthew 3
4. Genesis 10-12	Matthew 4
5. Genesis 13-15	Matthew 5:1-26
6. Genesis 16-17	Matthew 5:27-48
7. Genesis 18-19	Matthew 6:1-18
8. Genesis 20-22	Matthew 6:19-34
9. Genesis 23-24	Matthew 7
10. Genesis 25-26	Matthew 8:1-13
11. Genesis 27-28	Matthew 8:14-34
12. Genesis 29-30	Matthew 9:1-17
13. Genesis 31-32	Matthew 9:18-38
14. Genesis 33-35	Matther 10:1-15
15. Genesis 36-38	Matthew 10:16-42
16. Genesis 39-40	Matthew 11
17. Genesis 41-42	Matthew 12: 1 -24
18. Genesis 43-45	Matthew 12:25-50
19. Genesis 46-48	Matthew 13:1-30
20. Genesis 49-50	Matthew 13:31-58
21. Exodus 1-3	Matthew 14:1-21
22. Exodus 4-6	Matthew 14:22-36
23. Exodus 7-8	Matthew 15:1-20
24. Exodus 9-11	Matthew 15:21-39
25. Exodus 12-13	Matthew 16
26. Exodus 14-15	Matthew 17
27. Exodus 16-18	Matthew 18:1-20
28. Exodus 19-20	Matthew 18:21-35
29. Exodus 21-22	Matthew 19
30. Exodus 23-24	Matthew 20:1-16
31. Exodus 25-26	Matthew 20:17-34

February

1. Exodus 27-28	Mathew 21: 1-22
2. Exodus 29-30	Matthew 21:23-46
3. Exodus 31-33	Matthew 22:1-22
4. Exodus 34-35	Matthew 22: 23-46
5. Exodus 36-38	Matthew 23:1-22
6. Exodus 39-40	Matthew 23:23-39
7. Leviticus 1-3	Matthew 24:1-28
8. Leviticus 4-4	Matthew 24:29-51
9. Leviticus 6-7	Matthew 25:1-30
10. Leviticus 8-10	Matthew 25:31-46
11. Leviticus 11-12	Matthew 26:1-25
12. Leviticus 13	Matthew 26:26-50
13. Leviticus 14	Matthew 26 :51-75
14. Leviticus 15-16	Matthew 27:1-26
15. Leviticus 17-18	Matthew 27:27-50
16. Leviticus 19-20	Matthew 27:51-66
17. Leviticus 21-22	Matthew 28
18. Leviticus 23-24	Mark 1:1- 22
19. Leviticus 25	Mark 1: 23- 45
20. Leviticus 26-27	Mark 2
21. Number 1-2	Mark 3:1- 21
22. Number 3-4	Mark 3:22-35
23. Number 5-6	Mark 4:1-20
24. number 7-8	Mark 4:21-41
25. Number 9-11	Mark 5:1-20
26. Number 12-14	Mark 5:21-43
27. Number 15-16	Mark 6:1-29
28. Number 17-19	Mark 6:30-56

ONE YEAR BIBLE READING PLAN

March

1. Numbers 20-22 — Mark 7:1-13
2. Number 23-25 — Mark 7:14-37
3. Number 26-28 — Mark 8
4. Number 29-31 — Mark 9:1-29
5. Number 32-34 — Mark 9:30-50
6. Number 35-36 — Mark 10:1-31
7. Deuteronomy 1-3 — Mark 10:32-52
8. Deuteronomy 4-6 — Mark 11:1-18
9. Deuteronomy 7-9 — Mark 11:19-33
10. Deuteronomy 10-12 — Mark 12:1-27
11. Deuteronomy 13-15 — Mark 12:28-44
12. Deuteronomy 16-18 — Mark 13:1-20
13. Deuteronomy 19-21 — Mark 13:21-37
14. Deuteronomy 22-24 — Mark 14:1-26
15. Deuteronomy 25-27 — Mark 14:27-53
16. Deuteronomy 28-29 — Mark 14:54-72
17. Deuteronomy 30-31 — Mark 15:1-25
18. Deuteronomy 32-34 — Mark 15:26-47
19. Joshua 1-3 — Mark 16
20. Joshua 4-6 — Luke 1:1-20
21. Joshua 7-9 — Luke 1:21-38
22. Joshua 10-12 — Luke 1:39-56
23. Joshua 13-15 — Luke 1:57-80
24. Joshua 16-18 — Luke 2:1-24
25. Joshua 19-21 — Luke 2:25-52
26. Joshua 22-24 — Luke 3
27. Judges 1-3 — luke 4:1-30
28. Judges 4-6 — Luke 4:31-44
29. Judges 7-8 — Luke 5:1-16
30. Judges 9-10 — Luke 5:17-39
31. Judges 11-12 — Luke 6:1-23

April

1. Judges 13-15 — Luke 6:24-49
2. Judges16-18 — Luke 7:1-30
3. Judges 19-21 — Luke 7:31-50
4. Ruth 1-4 — Luke 8:1-25
5. I Samuel 1-3 — Luke 8:26-56
6. I Samuel 4-6 — Luke 9:1-17
7. I Samuel 7-9 — Luke 9:18-36
8. 1Samuel 10-12 — Luke 9:37-62
9. 1Samuel 13-14 — Luke 10:1-24
10. 1Samuel 15-16 — Luke 10:25-42
11. 1Samuel 17-18 — Luke 11:1-28
12. 1Samuel 19-21 — Luke 11:29-54
13. 1Samuel 22-24 — Luke 12:1-31
14. 1Samuel 25-26 — Luke 12:32-59
15. 1Samuel 27-29 — Luke 13:1-21
16. 1Samuel 30-31 — Luke 13:22-35
17. II Samuel 1-2 — Luke 14:1-24
18. II Samuel 3-5 — Luke 14:25-35
19. II Samuel 6-8 — Luke 15:1-10
20. II Samuel 9-11 — Luke 15:11-32
21. II Samuel 12-13 — Luke 16
22. II Samuel 14-15 — Luke 17:1-19
23. II Samuel 16-18 — Luke 17:20-37
24. II Samuel 19-20 — Luke 18:1-23
25. II Samuel 21-22 — Luke 18:24-43
26. II Samuel 23-24 — Luke 19:1-27
27. I Kings 1-2 — Luke 19:28-48
28. I Kings 3-5 — Luke 20:1-26
29. I Kings 6-7 — Luke 20:27-47
30. I Kings 8-9 — Luke 21:1-19

ONE YEAR BIBLE READING PLAN

May

1. I Kings 10-11 — Luke 21:20-38
2. I Kings 12-13 — Luke 22:1-30
3. I Kings 14-15 — Luke 22:31-46
4. I Kings 16-18 — Luke 22:47-71
5. I Kings 19-20 — Luke 23:1-26
6. I Kings 21-22 — Luke 23:27-56
7. II Kings 1-3 — Luke 24:1-35
8. II Kings 4-6 — Luke 24:36-53
9. II Kings 7-9 — John 1:1-28
10. II Kings 10-12 — John 1:29-51
11. II Kings 13-14 — John 2
12. II Kings 15-16 — John 3:1-22
13. II Kings 17-18 — John 3:23-36
14. II Kings 19-20 — John 4:1-30
15. II Kings 21-23 — John 4: 31-54
16. II Kings 24-25 — John 5:1-18
17. I Chronicles 1-3 — John 5:19-47
18. I Chronicles 4-6 — John 6:1-21
19. I Chronicles 7-9 — John 6:22-42
20. I Chronicles 10-12 — John 6:43-71
21. I Chronicles 13-15 — John 7:1-27
22. I Chronicles 16-18 — John 7:28-53
23. I Chronicles 19-21 — John 8:1-27
24. I Chronicles 22-24 — John 8:28-59
25. I Chronicles 25-27 — John 9:1-23
26. I Chronicles 28-29 — John 9:24-41
27. II Chronicles 1-3 — John 10:1-23
28. II Chronicles 4-6 — John 10:24-42
29. II Chronicles 7-9 — John 11:1-29
30. II Chronicles 10-12 — John 11:30-57
31. II Chronicles 13-14 — John 12:1-28

June

1. II Chronicles 15-16 — John 12:29-50
2. II Chronicles 17-18 — John 13:1-20
3. II Chronicles 19-20 — John 13:21-28
4. II Chronicles 21-22 — John 14
5. II Chronicles 23-24 — John 15
6. II Chronicles 25-27 — John 16
7. II Chronicles 28-29 — John 17
8. II Chronicles 30-31 — John 18:1-18
9. II Chronicles 32-33 — John 18:19-40
10. II Chronicles 34-36 — John 19:1-22
11. Ezra 1-2 — John 19:23-42
12. Ezra 3-5 — John 20
13. Ezra 6-8 — John 21
14. Ezra 9-10 — Acts 1
15. Nehemiah 1-3 — Acts 2:1-21
16. Nehemiah 4-6 — Acts 2:22-47
17. Nehemiah 7-9 — Acts 3
18. Nehemiah 10-11 — Acts 4:1-22
19. Nehemiah 12-13 — Acts 4:23-47
20. Esther 1-2 — Acts 5:1-25
21. Esther 3-5 — Acts 5:26-42
22. Esther 6-8 — Acts 6
23. Esther 9-10 — Acts 7:1-21
24. Job 1-2 — Acts 7: 22-43
25. Job 3-4 — Acts 7:44-60
26. Job 5-7 — Acts 8:1-25
27. Job 8-10 — Acts 8:26-40
28. Job 11-13 — Acts 9:1-21
29. Job 14-16 — Acts 9:22-43
30. Job 17-19 — Acts 10:1-23

ONE YEAR BIBLE READING PLAN

July

1. Job 20-21 — Acts 10:24-48
2. Job 22-24 — Acts 11
3. Job 25-27 — Acts 12
4. Job 28-29 — Acts 13:1-26
5. Job 30-31 — Acts 13:27-52
6. Job 32-33 — Acts 14
7. Job 34-35 — Acts 15:1-21
8. Job 36-37 — Acts 15:22-41
9. Job 38-40 — Acts 16:1-21
10. Job 41-42 — Acts 16:22-40
11. Psalm 1-3 — Acts 17:1-15
12. Psalm 4-6 — Acts 17:16-34
13. Psalm 7-9 — Acts 18
14. Psalm 10-12 — Acts 19:1-20
15. Psalm 13-15 — Acts 19:21-41
16. Psalm 16-17 — Acts 20:1-16
17. Psalm 18-19 — Acts 20:17-38
18. Psalm 20-22 — Acts 21:1-17
19. Psalm 23-25 — Acts 21:18-40
20. Psalm 26-28 — Acts 22
21. Psalm 29-30 — Acts 23:1-18
22. Psalm 31-32 — Acts 23:19-35
23. Psalm 33-34 — Acts 24
24. Psalm 35-36 — Acts 25
25. Psalm 37-39 — Acts 26
26. Psalm 40-42 — Acts 27:1-26
27. Psalm 43-45 — Acts 27:27-44
28. Psalm 46-48 — Acts 28
29. Psalm 49-50 — Romans 1
30. Psalm 51-53 — Romans 2
31. Psalm 54-56 — Romans 3

August

1. Psalm 57-59 — Romans 4
2. Psalm 60-62 — Romans 5
3. Psalm 63-65 — Romans 6
4. Psalm 66-67 — Romans 7
5. Psalm 68-69 — Romans 8:1-21
6. Psalm 70-71 — Romans 8:22-39
7. Psalm 72-73 — Romans 9:1-15
8. Psalm 74-76 — Romans 9:16-33
9. Psalm 77-78 — Romans 10
10. Psalm 79-80 — Romans 11:1-18
11. Psalm 81-83 — Romans 11:19-36
12. Psalm 84-86 — Romans 12
13. Psalm 87-88 — Romans 13
14. Psalm 89-90 — Romans 14
15. Psalm 91-93 — Romans 15:1-13
16. Psalm 94-96 — Romans 15:14-33
17. Psalm 97-99 — Romans 16
18. Psalm 100-102 — I Corinthians 1
19. Psalm 103-104 — I Corinthians 2
20. Psalm 105-106 — I Corinthians 3
21. Psalm 107-109 — I Corinthians 4
22. Psalm 110-112 — I Corinthians 5
23. Psalm 113-115 — I Corinthians 6
24. Psalm 116-118 — I Corinthians 7:1-19
25. Psalm 119:1-88 — I Corinthians 7:20-40
26. Psalm 119:89-176 — I Corinthians 8
27. Psalm 120-122 — I Corinthians 9
28. Psalm 123-125 — I Corinthians 10:1-18
29. Psalm 126-128 — I Corinthians 10:19-33
30. Psalm 129-131 — I Corinthians 11:1-16
31. Psalm 132-134 — I Corinthians 11:17-34

ONE YEAR BIBLE READING PLAN

September

1. Psalm 135-136	I Corinthians 12
2. Psalm 137-139	I Corinthians 13
3. Psalm 140-142	I Corinthians 14:1-20
4. Psalm 143-145	I Corinthians 14:21-40
5. Psalm 146-147	I Corinthians 15:1-28
6. Psalm 148-150	I Corinthians 15:29-58
7. Proverbs 1-2	I Corinthians 16
8. Provers 3-5	II Corinthians 1
9. Proverbs 6-7	II Corinthians 2
10. Proverbs 8-9	II Corinthians 3
11. Proverbs 10-12	II Corinthians 4
12. Proverbs 13-15	II Corinthians 5
13. Proverbs 16-18	II Corinthians 6
14. Proverbs 19-21	II Corinthians 7
15. Proverbs 22-24	II Corinthians 8
16. Proverbs 25-26	II Corinthians 9
17. Proverbs 27-29	II Corinthians 10
18. Proverbs 30-31	II Corinthians 11:1-15
19. Ecclesiastes 1-3	II Corinthians 11:16-33
20. Ecclesiastes 4-6	II Corinthians 12
21. Ecclesiastes 7-9	II Corinthians 13
22. Ecclesiastes 10-12	Galatians 1
23. Song of Solomon 1-3	Galatians 2
24. Song of Solomon 4-5	Galatians 3
25. Song of Solomon 6-8	Galatians 4
26. Isaiah 1-2	Galatians 5
27. Isaiah 3-4	Galatians 6
28. Isaiah 5-6	Ephesians 1
29. Isaiah 7-8	Ephesians 2
30. Isaiah 9-10	Ephesians 3

October

1. Isaiah 11-13	Ephesians 4
2. Isaiah 14-16	Ephesians 5:1-16
3. Isaiah 17-19	Ephesians 5:17-33
4. Isaiah 20-22	Ephesians 6
5. Isaiah 23-25	Philippians 1
6. Isaiah 26-28	Philippians 2
7. Isaiah 29-31	Philippians 3
8. Isaiah 32-34	Philippians 4
9. Isaiah 35-37	Colossians 1
10. Isaiah 38-41	Colossians 2
11. Isaiah 42-45	Colossians 3
12. Isaiah 46-49	Colossians 4
13. Isaiah 50-52	I Thessalonians 1
14. Isaiah 53-56	I Thessalonians 2
15. Isaiah 57-59	I Thessalonians 3
16. Isaiah 60-63	I Thessalonians 4
17. Isaiah 64-66	I Thessalonians 5
18. Jeremiah 1-2	II Thessalonians 1
19. Jeremiah 3-4	II Thessalonians 2
20. Jeremiah 5-7	II Thessalonians 3
21. Jeremiah 8-9	I Timothy 1
22. Jeremiah 10-12	I Timothy 2
23. Jeremiah 13-15	I Timothy 3
24. Jeremiah 16-18	I Timothy 4
25. Jeremiah 19-22	I Timothy 5
26. Jeremiah 23-25	I Timothy 6
27. Jeremiah 26-28	II Timothy 1
28. Jeremiah 29-31	II Timothy 2
29. Jeremiah 32-34	II Timothy 3
30. Jeremiah 35-38	II Timothy 3
31. Jeremiah 39-41	Titus 1

ONE YEAR BIBLE READING PLAN

November

1. Jeremiah 42-43   Titus 2
2. Jeremiah 44-47   Titus 3
3. Jeremiah 48-50   Philemon
4. Jeremiah 51-52   Hebrews 1
5. Lamentations 1-2   Hebrews 2
6. Lamentations 3-5   Hebrews 3
7. Ezekiel 1-2   Hebrews 4
8. Ezekiel 3-5   Hebrews 5
9. Ezekiel 6-7   Hebrews 6
10. Ezekiel 8-10   Hebrews 7
11. Ezekiel 11-12   Hebrews 8
12. Ezekiel 13-14   Hebrews 9
13. Ezekiel 15-16   Hebrews 10
14. Ezekiel 17-18   Hebrews 11
15. Ezekiel 19-20   Hebrews 12
16. Ezekiel 21-22   Hebrews 13
17. Ezekiel 23-24   James 1
18. Ezekiel 25-26   James 2
19. Ezekiel 27-28   James 3
20. Ezekiel 29-30   James 4
21. Ezekiel 31-32   James 5
22. Ezekiel 33-34   1 Peter 1
23. Ezekiel 35-36   I Peter 2
24. Ezekiel 37-38   I Peter 3
25. Ezekiel 39-40   I Peter 4
26. Ezekiel 41-42   I Peter 5
27. Ezekiel 43-44   II Peter 1
28. Ezekiel 45-46   II Peter 2
29. Ezekiel 47   II Peter 3
30. Ezekiel 48   II John 1

December

1. Daniel 1-3   I John 2
2. Daniel 4-6   I John 3
3. Daniel 7-9   I John 4
4. Daniel 10-12   I John 5
5. Hosea 1-4   II John
6. Hosea 5-8   III John
7. Hosea 9-11   Jude
8. Hosea 12-14   Revelation 1
9. Joel 1-2   Revelation 2
10. Joel 3   Revelation 3
11. Amos 1-2   Revelation 4
12. Amos 3-4   Revelation 5
13. Amos 5-6   Revelation 6
14. Amos 7-9   Revelation 7
15. Obadiah   Revelation 8
16. Jonah 1-2   Revelation 9
17. Jonah 3-4   Revelation 10
18. Micah 1-3   Revelation 11
19. Micah 4-6   Revelation 12
20. Micah 7   Revelation 13
21. Nahum 1-3   Revelation 14
22. Habakkuk 1-2   Revelation 15
23. Habakkuk 3   Revelation 16
24. Zephaniah 1-3   Revelation 17
25. Haggai 1-2   Revelation 18:1-10
26. Zechariah 1-4   Revelation 18:11-24
27. Zechariah 5-8   Revelation 19
28. Zechariah 9-11   Revelation 20
29. Zechariah 12-14   Revelation 21:1-13
30. Malachi 1-2   Revelation 21:14-27
31. Malachi 3-4   Revelation 22

A morning prayer- Father I pray that my relationship with You will reach a higher level. Breath on me, refresh my soul, help me to see myself and others the way that You do. Help me to be more like You every day. Thank you for Your great mercy and grace.

_____

_____

_____

_____

_____

_____

_____

_____

_____

_____

_____

_____

_____

_____

_____

Determine every day to overcome evil with good and decrease the darkness with the light of God's goodness through His word.

_____

_____

_____

_____

_____

_____

_____

_____

_____

_____

_____

_____

_____

_____

_____

_____

What you meditate on will control the path of your life. There is power in focus.

_____

_____

_____

_____

_____

_____

_____

_____

_____

_____

_____

_____

_____

_____

_____

_____

_____

In the midst of brokenness there is still hope.

_____

_____

_____

_____

_____

_____

_____

_____

_____

_____

_____

_____

_____

_____

_____

_____

The same God that numbered the sand on the seashore and the stars in the sky is the same God that lives inside of you. He hears your prayers.

_____

_____

_____

_____

_____

_____

_____

_____

_____

_____

_____

_____

_____

_____

_____

_____

Open ears to the word of God are closed ears to all that will distract.

_____

_____

_____

_____

_____

_____

_____

_____

_____

_____

_____

_____

_____

_____

_____

_____

The Word of God activated is the most powerful force in the universe. It will completely change lives.

_____

_____

_____

_____

_____

_____

_____

_____

_____

_____

_____

_____

_____

_____

_____

_____

_____

Take every word that God speaks to you and use those words to form the atmosphere of heaven in your life on the earth.

_____

_____

_____

_____

_____

_____

_____

_____

_____

_____

_____

_____

_____

_____

_____

_____

_____

Trust God in the challenge.

_____

_____

_____

_____

_____

_____

_____

_____

_____

_____

_____

_____

_____

_____

_____

_____

_____

Live life in the most radiant of hues.

You are made for a purpose on purpose.

_____

_____

_____

_____

_____

_____

_____

_____

_____

_____

_____

_____

_____

_____

_____

_____

If you find yourself asking God where is He, remember He will never leave or forsake you.

_____

_____

_____

_____

_____

_____

_____

_____

_____

_____

_____

_____

_____

_____

_____

_____

Your validation will not come through tweets, post, social media, money or other people. When you make Jesus Lord, He will validate you.

_____

_____

_____

_____

_____

_____

_____

_____

_____

_____

_____

_____

_____

_____

_____

_____

_____

In Genesis 27:42 Rebekah told Jacob that Esau comforted himself by planning to kill him. Beware of the comfort that is found in being offended. Choose the comfort of The Holy Spirit instead and release any offense against others.

_____

_____

_____

_____

_____

_____

_____

_____

_____

_____

_____

_____

_____

_____

_____

Sometimes simply saying I'm sorry can heal a hurt.

Made by God, loved by God, called by God is who you are. Walk in your identity.

_____

_____

_____

_____

_____

_____

_____

_____

_____

_____

_____

_____

_____

_____

_____

_____

Put your past, present and future in God's hands, trust the process and keep it moving.

_____

_____

_____

_____

_____

_____

_____

_____

_____

_____

_____

_____

_____

_____

_____

_____

_____

Mind your thoughts and mind your business by giving the mind of Christ priority.

We reap what we sow. Sow love not hate, sow peace not drama, sow kindness not cruelty.

_____

_____

_____

_____

_____

_____

_____

_____

_____

_____

_____

_____

_____

_____

_____

_____

_____

Instead of stressing and worrying, choose to rest in the Great I Am.

_____

_____

_____

_____

_____

_____

_____

_____

_____

_____

_____

_____

_____

_____

_____

_____

Faith compels you to become doers of God's word. Actions are a result of beliefs.

Jesus is the Lion and the Lamb. He is the One who fights your battles and the One Who brings comfort.

_____

_____

_____

_____

_____

_____

_____

_____

_____

_____

_____

_____

_____

_____

_____

_____

God has made a way to escape every temptation so you can avoid unnecessary danger.

_____

_____

_____

_____

_____

_____

_____

_____

_____

_____

_____

_____

_____

_____

_____

_____

_____

_____

_____

Obeying the Lord does not guarantee favor with man but God's approval outweighs all others.

_____

_____

_____

_____

_____

_____

_____

_____

_____

_____

_____

_____

_____

_____

_____

_____

Believe in yourself even when others do not. Keep it moving and they will catch up.

_____

_____

_____

_____

_____

_____

_____

_____

_____

_____

_____

_____

_____

_____

_____

_____

_____

Jesus said to come to Him when you are weighed down and He will give you rest. If you are weary, tell Him, if you are overburdened tell Him and expect to be refreshed.

_____

_____

_____

_____

_____

_____

_____

_____

_____

_____

_____

_____

_____

_____

_____

_____

Believe the best. Everything is going to be ok.

Never allow the struggles in life to convince you that Jesus is not enough.

You are blessed and highly favored. Have a great day!

_____

_____

_____

_____

_____

_____

_____

_____

_____

_____

_____

_____

_____

_____

_____

_____

_____

King Saul spent much of his time chasing after David to harm him while David spent much of his time chasing after God writing Psalms to Him. Don't waste your time on fruitless endeavors. Stay focused.

_____

_____

_____

_____

_____

_____

_____

_____

_____

_____

_____

_____

_____

_____

_____

_____

The Comfort of the Holy Spirit is pure and undeniable. Do not be stressed, be comforted.

_____

_____

_____

_____

_____

_____

_____

_____

_____

_____

_____

_____

_____

_____

_____

_____

_____

_____

God has graced you to be who you are. Comparing yourself to others is fruitless.

_____

_____

_____

_____

_____

_____

_____

_____

_____

_____

_____

_____

_____

_____

_____

_____

You were made in God's image according to His blueprint. You are an original so stay in your lane.

_____

_____

_____

_____

_____

_____

_____

_____

_____

_____

_____

_____

_____

_____

_____

_____

Everything will be ok. I AM THAT I AM is all you need.

_____

_____

_____

_____

_____

_____

_____

_____

_____

_____

_____

_____

_____

_____

_____

_____

_____

Just because something is not easy does not mean that God is not in it.

_____

_____

_____

_____

_____

_____

_____

_____

_____

_____

_____

_____

_____

_____

_____

_____

_____

_____

If you are having a challenging day do not grow weary. Turn it over to God. This too shall pass.

_____

_____

_____

_____

_____

_____

_____

_____

_____

_____

_____

_____

_____

_____

_____

_____

You can be a vessel in healing others. Healing can be found in a kind gesture, a compassionate look and a gentle word.

_____

_____

_____

_____

_____

_____

_____

_____

_____

_____

_____

_____

_____

_____

_____

Today is a new day, let your light shine!

_____

_____

_____

_____

_____

_____

_____

_____

_____

_____

_____

_____

_____

_____

_____

_____

_____

You are more than a conqueror through Him that loves you. Victory is your birthright.

_____

_____

_____

_____

_____

_____

_____

_____

_____

_____

_____

_____

_____

_____

_____

_____

Expect to see God's amazing grace in your life.

The hustle is real and so is hearing God's voice. Take time everyday to stop and listen.

_____

_____

_____

_____

_____

_____

_____

_____

_____

_____

_____

_____

_____

_____

_____

_____

_____

Embrace the word of God and allow it to form the atmosphere of heaven all around you.

_____

_____

_____

_____

_____

_____

_____

_____

_____

_____

_____

_____

_____

_____

_____

_____

Walking in Gods grace, power and humility will produce His kingdom in the earth. There is power in every likeness of God in your life.

_____

_____

_____

_____

_____

_____

_____

_____

_____

_____

_____

_____

_____

_____

_____

_____

_____

_____

The voice of The Lord is powerful. His voice has the power to strengthen you, release peace into your soul, change circumstances and produce positive results.

_____
_____
_____
_____
_____
_____
_____
_____
_____
_____
_____
_____
_____
_____
_____
_____

Do not allow criticism of others to take your soul somewhere God did not send you.

_____

_____

_____

_____

_____

_____

_____

_____

_____

_____

_____

_____

_____

_____

_____

_____

_____

God is trustworthy, hold on, He is very present help in trouble.

_____

_____

_____

_____

_____

_____

_____

_____

_____

_____

_____

_____

_____

_____

_____

_____

God is doing something amazing for you. Trust him.

The word of God is a living force. It is powerful enough to change hearts.

_____

_____

_____

_____

_____

_____

_____

_____

_____

_____

_____

_____

_____

_____

_____

Grace will cause you not to be moved by things that once annoyed you.

_____

_____

_____

_____

_____

_____

_____

_____

_____

_____

_____

_____

_____

_____

_____

_____

God's Word teaches us how to live above the chaos of life and into the stillness of His presence.

_____

_____

_____

_____

_____

_____

_____

_____

_____

_____

_____

_____

_____

_____

_____

_____

To forgive brings great gain.

_____

_____

_____

_____

_____

_____

_____

_____

_____

_____

_____

_____

_____

_____

_____

_____

_____

_____

The Lord is The Alpha and Omega. If He started it He will finish it.

_____

_____

_____

_____

_____

_____

_____

_____

_____

_____

_____

_____

_____

_____

_____

_____

_____

God will give you His thoughts. You are responsible to see His thoughts as valuable and position them above all other thoughts.

_____

_____

_____

_____

_____

_____

_____

_____

_____

_____

_____

_____

_____

_____

_____

_____

God gives insight , revelation knowledge, good understanding and a renewed mind. Thank you Lord for your amazing grace.

_____

_____

_____

_____

_____

_____

_____

_____

_____

_____

_____

_____

_____

_____

_____

A Daily Prayer- Lord teach met to love like I ought to love

Help me to think like I ought to think

Help me to judge with Your righteous judgement

Give me the knowledge I need to succeed

Lead me in Your divine path

Help me to speak words from Your heart

Make me a blessing to others

Help me to see from Your perspective

You are the Lord of my life.

_____

_____

_____

_____

_____

_____

_____

_____

_____

_____

The gifts and talents that God gives are for His glory and will also help others.

_____

_____

_____

_____

_____

_____

_____

_____

_____

_____

_____

_____

_____

_____

_____

_____

_____

Whatever your purpose is, know that you have been fearfully and wonderfully made.

_____

_____

_____

_____

_____

_____

_____

_____

_____

_____

_____

_____

_____

_____

_____

_____

_____

_____

God is the author of your life's purpose and that is where success can be found. Your life is significant, you matter.

_____

_____

_____

_____

_____

_____

_____

_____

_____

_____

_____

_____

_____

_____

_____

_____

Accepting truth is a choice.

_____

_____

_____

_____

_____

_____

_____

_____

_____

_____

_____

_____

_____

_____

_____

_____

_____

The enemy comes to steal valuable things like love, joy, peace, kindness, patience, self control, faithfulness and humility. All of those things are part of God's abundant life for you. Guard your valuables.

_____

_____

_____

_____

_____

_____

_____

_____

_____

_____

_____

_____

_____

_____

_____

_____

Do not be fearful or discouraged over what you do not have. Take what you do have and do so as Jesus did with the few loaves and fish, lift it up to heaven and give thanks.

On difficult days determine to set your mind on things above, move forward and remind yourself you are hidden in Christ.

The Lord is rooting for you to succeed. His prayer is that your faith will not fail.

_____

_____

_____

_____

_____

_____

_____

_____

_____

_____

_____

_____

_____

_____

_____

_____

You are made in His image. Know your worth and never settle.

Truth is to be treasured.

The abundant life is not a life void of challenges but one where the grace of God is operative to overcome the challenges.

_____

_____

_____

_____

_____

_____

_____

_____

_____

_____

_____

_____

_____

_____

_____

_____

_____

No one can fill the barren places inside of you the way God does with such hope and purpose.

_____

_____

_____

_____

_____

_____

_____

_____

_____

_____

_____

_____

_____

_____

_____

_____

_____

God will fill you to the level of your hunger and thirst. Hunger and thirst after righteousness and you will be filled.

_____

_____

_____

_____

_____

_____

_____

_____

_____

_____

_____

_____

_____

_____

_____

_____

David's brother Eliab accused David of having an evil heart but God said it was Eliab's heart that was not right. The accusations we make about others should alert us to check our own heart.

_____

_____

_____

_____

_____

_____

_____

_____

_____

_____

_____

_____

_____

_____

_____

_____

_____

Love changes people. God is love.

_____

_____

_____

_____

_____

_____

_____

_____

_____

_____

_____

_____

_____

_____

_____

_____

Trusting God is like a fortified wall repelling things sent to harm it.

_____

_____

_____

_____

_____

_____

_____

_____

_____

_____

_____

_____

_____

_____

_____

_____

_____

_____

_____

When we see ourselves through God's perspective, we find ourselves free to love ourselves and others as God loves us.

_____

_____

_____

_____

_____

_____

_____

_____

_____

_____

_____

_____

_____

_____

_____

_____

You are tattooed on God's hand and your name is written in His book of remembrance. You are forever on His mind.

_____

_____

_____

_____

_____

_____

_____

_____

_____

_____

_____

_____

_____

_____

_____

_____

_____

_____

When all is said and done only what we do for Christ will matter. Live each day with His purpose.

_____

_____

_____

_____

_____

_____

_____

_____

_____

_____

_____

_____

_____

_____

_____

_____

_____

If you find yourself feeling offended, provoked, bitter, hurt or any negative emotion, remind yourself that this is an opportunity to get closer to God. Be strengthened by Him and mature spiritually.

_____

_____

_____

_____

_____

_____

_____

_____

_____

_____

_____

_____

_____

_____

_____

_____

_____

Seeking the Lord and His Kingdom first will always impact your life in a good way.

_____

_____

_____

_____

_____

_____

_____

_____

_____

_____

_____

_____

_____

_____

_____

_____

Speak words of truth and significance in the world and silence the opposition.

God knows every trial you will face in life. He is never caught off guard or surprised. His grace is always enough. You got this!

_____

_____

_____

_____

_____

_____

_____

_____

_____

_____

_____

_____

_____

_____

_____

_____

_____

Jesus paid the price for us to disconnect from negative things in order to abide and connect with Him. Determine to live your life above negativity, live the abundant life.

_____

_____

_____

_____

_____

_____

_____

_____

_____

_____

_____

_____

_____

_____

_____

_____

_____

_____

According to the Word of God Esther was very beautiful. Her beauty stood out for a purpose. Even outward appearances are orchestrated with a divine purpose.

_____

_____

_____

_____

_____

_____

_____

_____

_____

_____

_____

_____

_____

_____

_____

_____

One can idolize people and things. When God's purpose is given priority, idols are put in their proper place.

_____

_____

_____

_____

_____

_____

_____

_____

_____

_____

_____

_____

_____

_____

_____

_____

_____

Making comparisons can be a trap. What God has for you is for you.

_____

_____

_____

_____

_____

_____

_____

_____

_____

_____

_____

_____

_____

_____

_____

When we give God our time. He gives us His strength. Such a great exchange.

_____

_____

_____

_____

_____

_____

_____

_____

_____

_____

_____

_____

_____

_____

_____

_____

_____

Love has a certain attitude, a certain behavior and a certain way of speaking. It can be seen, heard and felt. Love looks like something.

_____

_____

_____

_____

_____

_____

_____

_____

_____

_____

_____

_____

_____

_____

_____

_____

The Bible speaks of setting aside the things that so easily besets us. God will take the things that most annoy, intimidate and harass us and strengthen us in every weakness.

_____

_____

_____

_____

_____

_____

_____

_____

_____

_____

_____

_____

_____

_____

_____

Come boldly to the throne of grace because boldness represents confidence that God will hear and answer you.

Samson's strength felt natural to him until he no longer possessed it. Grace enables us to do what we cannot do on our own.

_____

_____

_____

_____

_____

_____

_____

_____

_____

_____

_____

_____

_____

_____

_____

_____

_____

Hate, strife, pride or unforgiveness has never won a battle against the Word of God. If God said it, believe it.

_____

_____

_____

_____

_____

_____

_____

_____

_____

_____

_____

_____

_____

_____

_____

_____

When you work with God through obedience, you are guaranteed the God kind of success. Good success.

_____

_____

_____

_____

_____

_____

_____

_____

_____

_____

_____

_____

_____

_____

_____

_____

_____

_____

David strengthened himself in the Lord. All the real strength you possess comes from the Lord.

_____

_____

_____

_____

_____

_____

_____

_____

_____

_____

_____

_____

_____

_____

_____

_____

Let the seeds that you sow be worth reaping.

_____

_____

_____

_____

_____

_____

_____

_____

_____

_____

_____

_____

_____

_____

_____

_____

_____

There is not much wiggle room on the narrow road but it is the most prosperous way to live.

_____

_____

_____

_____

_____

_____

_____

_____

_____

_____

_____

_____

_____

_____

_____

Forgiveness opens doors to the miraculous.

_____

_____

_____

_____

_____

_____

_____

_____

_____

_____

_____

_____

_____

_____

_____

_____

_____

When God tells you something believe Him.

_____

_____

_____

_____

_____

_____

_____

_____

_____

_____

_____

_____

_____

_____

_____

_____

_____

Mirror mirror on the wall, who am I and what is my call? The more you look into the mirror of God's Word and His promises you will reflect and become who He has called you to be.

_____

_____

_____

_____

_____

_____

_____

_____

_____

_____

_____

_____

_____

_____

Tenacity keeps knocking, keeps praying keeps believing and never gives up.

_____

_____

_____

_____

_____

_____

_____

_____

_____

_____

_____

_____

_____

_____

_____

_____

_____

Setting boundaries is a necessity. Guard your heart.

_____

_____

_____

_____

_____

_____

_____

_____

_____

_____

_____

_____

_____

_____

_____

_____

_____

When you are discouraged, or sad, His joy and victorious anointing is available to make an exchange.

_____

_____

_____

_____

_____

_____

_____

_____

_____

_____

_____

_____

_____

_____

_____

_____

Spiritual battles are never won using carnal weapons.

_____

_____

_____

_____

_____

_____

_____

_____

_____

_____

_____

_____

_____

_____

_____

_____

_____

Repentance is God's idea and it is brilliant.

_____

_____

_____

_____

_____

_____

_____

_____

_____

_____

_____

_____

_____

_____

_____

_____

_____

Whatever is going on in your life today, whatever is going on in the world today, love is still the answer.

_____

_____

_____

_____

_____

_____

_____

_____

_____

_____

_____

_____

_____

_____

_____

You are God's shining precious gemstone. Remember your worth. Malachi 3:17

_____

_____

_____

_____

_____

_____

_____

_____

_____

_____

_____

_____

_____

_____

_____

_____

_____

Laugh hard, smile big, dance in the rain and never hold a grudge.

_____

_____

_____

_____

_____

_____

_____

_____

_____

_____

_____

_____

_____

_____

_____

_____

_____

Overcomers do not run, hide, quit, make excuses or blame others. They overcome.

_____

_____

_____

_____

_____

_____

_____

_____

_____

_____

_____

_____

_____

_____

_____

_____

_____

The name of God is never mentioned in the book of Esther yet we see God working mightily through and for His people. Even when you do not sense His presence, He is still there.

_____

_____

_____

_____

_____

_____

_____

_____

_____

_____

_____

_____

_____

_____

_____

_____

God made everything from nothing.

_____

_____

_____

_____

_____

_____

_____

_____

_____

_____

_____

_____

_____

_____

_____

_____

Love wins every struggle every time.

_____

_____

_____

_____

_____

_____

_____

_____

_____

_____

_____

_____

_____

_____

_____

_____

_____

Dying to self allows God's plan to prevail.

_____

_____

_____

_____

_____

_____

_____

_____

_____

_____

_____

_____

_____

_____

_____

_____

Make the Lord your Vanguard. He will always go before you and prepare the way.

There are thorns all around the rose stem but in spite of the thorns, the rose continues to bloom.

_____

_____

_____

_____

_____

_____

_____

_____

_____

_____

_____

_____

_____

_____

_____

Wisdom has been made available to you for every situation that you may face.

When we give God our trash, He gives us His treasure. Beauty for ashes.

_____

_____

_____

_____

_____

_____

_____

_____

_____

_____

_____

_____

_____

_____

_____

_____

_____

The power of God will take all the fragments and broken pieces of our lives and make us whole.

_____

_____

_____

_____

_____

_____

_____

_____

_____

_____

_____

_____

_____

_____

In every Garden of Eden there is a serpent suggesting that you question God's Word. Keep believing.

_____

_____

_____

_____

_____

_____

_____

_____

_____

_____

_____

_____

_____

_____

_____

Believing in the truth and walking in the truth will produce a pure heart, a clear conscience and genuine faith.

_____

_____

_____

_____

_____

_____

_____

_____

_____

_____

_____

_____

_____

_____

_____

_____

Every star is different, but they are together harmonious. When we accept one another's differences, we become harmonized diversity.

_____

_____

_____

_____

_____

_____

_____

_____

_____

_____

_____

_____

_____

_____

_____

_____

Knowing God is everything.

_____
_____
_____
_____
_____
_____
_____
_____
_____
_____
_____
_____
_____
_____
_____
_____
_____
_____

Do the right thing even when the wrong thing is easier.

_____

_____

_____

_____

_____

_____

_____

_____

_____

_____

_____

_____

_____

_____

_____

You are jewels valued and treasured. God calls you His own.

Our fears can be calmed with a thought, we can be uplifted with a thought, we can experience great victories with a thought. Keep your mind centered on The Lord.

_____

_____

_____

_____

_____

_____

_____

_____

_____

_____

_____

_____

_____

_____

_____

Do not be afraid to be all that you are called to be and allow others to do the same.

_____

_____

_____

_____

_____

_____

_____

_____

_____

_____

_____

_____

_____

_____

_____

_____

God is always right.

_____

_____

_____

_____

_____

_____

_____

_____

_____

_____

_____

_____

_____

_____

_____

_____

_____

_____

Have the courage to do something that seems hard. God works in spaces beyond ourselves.

The enemy's assignment is to get you to quit your assignment. Hang in there and remember that you are more than a conqueror.

_____

_____

_____

_____

_____

_____

_____

_____

_____

_____

_____

_____

_____

_____

_____

_____

Resolve to stay rooted because you must be rooted in order to bloom.

_____

_____

_____

_____

_____

_____

_____

_____

_____

_____

_____

_____

_____

_____

_____

_____

God's power is greater than your brokenness.

God would not promise you something that He will not make available to you. Believe and press with passion towards the goal that leads to possessing, attaining and walking in His character and nature.

_____

_____

_____

_____

_____

_____

_____

_____

_____

_____

_____

_____

_____

_____

_____

_____

Emerge into the calling of your Creator. Be a source of light that reflects wisdom and peace that comes from above.

_____

_____

_____

_____

_____

_____

_____

_____

_____

_____

_____

_____

_____

_____

_____

_____

_____

Forgive everyone that has hurt you, overcome the challenges and trust God.

_____

_____

_____

_____

_____

_____

_____

_____

_____

_____

_____

_____

_____

_____

_____

_____

_____

_____

God is thinking about you today.

_____

_____

_____

_____

_____

_____

_____

_____

_____

_____

_____

_____

_____

_____

_____

_____

Without love the world would be a very lonely place. Love one another.

The love of God is like liquid sunshine. It radiates into your heart and transforms your entire being. Let the Son-shine in!

_____

_____

_____

_____

_____

_____

_____

_____

_____

_____

_____

_____

_____

_____

_____

_____

An Evening Prayer-Father, as I reflect on the beauty of Your holiness, thank You for Your mercy and grace that helps me daily. Thank you for strengthening me for the journey and for teaching me how to laugh with true joy and rest in You.

_____

_____

_____

_____

_____

_____

_____

_____

_____

_____

_____

_____

_____

_____

_____